BALTHAZAR KORAB

COLUMBUS INDIANA

AN AMERICAN LANDMARK

to Monica

2

BALTHAZAR KORAB

COLUMBUS
INDIANA

AN AMERICAN LANDMARK

DOCUMAN PRESS

ACKNOWLEDGEMENTS

Laureates of awards routinely end their acceptance speeches with a long list of acknowledgements. If such proven experts feel the need to recognize their contributors, imagine how much I, a novice in publishing, owe my supporters. Lured by the illusion of total control, encouraged by slightly irresponsible friends, I decided to write, design, produce and publish this book all on my own — or so I thought. It turned out that a lot of help was needed and received. So when uttering the sentence that sounds somewhat hollow at Oscar ceremonies, "…and without their help I could not have done it," — believe me I mean it.

I could not have done it without the selfless, persistent support, encouragement and faith of Peggy Ann Charipar: Her involvement in multiple areas of the task, aided at times by her daughter Diane, earns her a lion's share in this work.

Thanks are due to many more for editorial and technical help and all other kinds of assistance. I am greatly indebted to my family and staff for their moral support that went far beyond all their practical involvements. In two years the book became a yoke, a demon, a vampire weighing heavily on our daily life. All the while Gary Quesada was valiantly holding down the fort.

Edward F. Sullivan with his wife Lynne embraced the cause of the book. He performed in many ways as head of the Heritage Fund providing an important liaison with the community.

Norman Carver, Jr. helped me through the aesthetic, technical and business matters of publishing. Thanks are due to Sylvia Sutton for her patient wrestling with my prose, to Jack Wyman for his delicately drawn plans, to Steven V. Roberts for graciously allowing me to quote from his *Esquire* article on J. Irwin Miller, and to Mrs. Clementine Tangeman and Mr. and Mrs. J. Irwin Miller for authorizing publication of their homes at some sacrifice to their privacy.

There was a lot of pleasure in my contacts with helpful people verifying the facts in the book. "Landmark on the Prairie," for instance, was my first subtitle. I liked it. It had panache, but it had to go. I was informed by Mrs. Miller that a climax forest once grew on these plains with nary a blade of grass in sight.

The sign "Athens on the Prairie" that once greeted visitors on route 46 was my one hope to save "prairie." But that fantasy of some eastern journalist has been since replaced by Rotary and Kiwanis emblems.

So I lost "prairie" but another compelling image was saved. I once photographed a log cabin built from the settlers' raft a good one hundred miles up the Ohio river in Kentucky. When I "floated" that idea downriver to southern Indiana my editor questioned the source. Thanks to historian Susanna Jones for validating my poetic license.

The County Offices, City Hall and the Library were of most valuable assistance. I listened to long stories from friends or random strangers. They gave me insight even if at times they were bordering on fiction.

Columbus stirs the imagination.

Thanks to every one. With their help my impressionist prose was "embellished by facts."

© 1989 Balthazar Korab   Designed by Balthazar Korab
ISBN 0.932076.20.3 cloth   ISBN 0.932076.21.1 paper
Printed in USA by Mossberg & Company Inc., 301 E. Sample St.
   P.O. Box 210, South Bend, IN 46624-0210.
Documan Press, Ltd., P.O. Box 387, Kalamazoo, Michigan 49005.
First Printing 1989

FOREWORD

Columbus is unique and inspires all residents, old and new. Following an architectural awareness symposium in 1983, co-sponsored by the Heritage Fund, Lisa Joy Wilson, a new resident wrote:

Columbus faithfully preserves its historical monuments and continues to build for its future.... Columbus architecture...gives hope and encouragement to all its citizens. It fosters life.

As a long-time resident, it has been my privilege to witness the positive influence of the architecture inspired by the leadership of J. Irwin Miller and the generous financial support of the Cummins Engine Foundation.

The Heritage Fund is excited about the publishing of this book. We feel that it is an appropriate time to encourage work of a true artist who has so beautifully recorded the physical development of this area that means so much to all of us.

W. Calvert Brand

W. Calvert Brand
Chairman & President
Heritage Fund of
Bartholomew County, Inc.

CONTENTS

PREFACE

Columbus is an improbable town. Every year scores of visitors arrive to pace its streets and study its buildings, for it is one of the rare places on earth where the idea that architecture can improve the human condition has been put to the test. How this small, southern Indiana community with no apparent call to destiny evolved into a unique landmark is a history that one day must be written.

I am not that historian. The history I offer is a tale told in images chosen from a body of work done over 30 years. The result may appear to be a book about architecture. But it is really the story of the people of Columbus who responded to the leadership of a family which had a great tradition in building, and to the voice of a man with vision.

If you look at a building as an organic shell expressing the character of its builders and its users, you will understand why I insist this is a book about people. Your examination will reaffirm the words of Winston Churchill: "We shape our buildings, and afterwards our buildings shape us."

The honor to publish this book has fallen to me. I do so with enthusiasm, but I must waive all claims to objectivity. Many of the people who helped build Columbus are my friends. I have a hopelessly sympathetic bias for this Indiana town.

INTONATION

"Give me a sky, a big sky, thirty-seven feet long and eight feet tall, something vast, the prairie, the cornfields — an unlimited horizon," said Cesar Pelli when he asked me to create a mural for a branch bank in the Commons.

I had to search for the right image for weeks, but finally the panels were installed, and a big sky it was. One curious onlooker noticed the silo peeking out among the cornstalks, and remarked, "Well, if it isn't the Stadler's field!" It was. And the Stadler's field was only about two miles from where its image stretched across the bank wall.

So it is in Columbus. The fields of corn and tobacco reach the floodplains, and at sunrise the shadow of the courthouse tower touches the fields.

In Columbus if you grow up fishing and hunting, you just might be able to hear your mother's call for dinner. The town nestles into the confluence of three creeks which limit the growth on the waterside, but not the fun. A lush green belt overlooking the elegant Cummins Headquarters that now occupies the site of the old railroad yards has become a favorite picnic grounds. There is growth, of course, to the east and the north, but the creek's natural boundary protects the core of the town. Routes 31 and 46 meander through that core like the creeks and the railroad giving the impression that the U.S. Surveyors' grid — which makes Iowa so dull and San Francisco so absurd — was dropped on Columbus as an afterthought. Yet once the grid had fallen, Columbus adopted it with gusto and dutifully named straight streets after Washington, Franklin, and Lafayette or, more plainly, after sycamores and elms. Most corners were confirmed by an accent: where no courthouse or city hall marks the block there stands a proud house, a church, a three-story building. The dignified old county courthouse, built in 1874, still dominates the landscape and speaks about the people who built it.

*Cornfields off Route 46: A study for a photographic mural for
an Irwin Union Branch Bank.*

Cornfields off Interstate 65.

What impetuous force drove those settlers of southern Indiana to build to last? They came across the Appalachians by wagon or down the Ohio by raft, built their first shelters with the timbers from their rafts, and soon replaced them with enduring structures of stone and brick. The urge to build solidly and handsomely was contagious, possibly something in the drinking water. All the settlers seemed to catch it, including the religious colonies such as the Rappites from New Harmony and the Shakers. Even while preparing for doomsday under a vow of chastity, they built buildings that still stand and set the norms for quality.

The impulse for quality has survived in Columbus. It is manifest in modern buildings, too, even in our age when too much building activity has been taken over by financial wizards, when the reality of "real" estate is calculated over twenty years of depreciation.

I flew over the Walesboro plant recently. A new angle to view this favorite building of mine, where an imaginative idea was stubbornly executed, even though common sense argued against a parking lot on the roof when there were so many wide open acres around. Because common sense lost the argument, workers from any point inside the plant sense themselves enclosed in a soft green curtain.

This preference for sterling values over expediency seems to be a key to an old puzzle of mine:

While working for Eero Saarinen I spent three whole months laboring over the design of a fireplace. It was frustrating. I was fresh from impoverished postwar Europe so such an extravaganza was indeed puzzling. So much energy spent on such a simple task! However, this particular fireplace was for Columbus. Knowing what I now know about this town, I understand.

One fine Sunday in March, before the tourist season had started, I found the gates of the Irwin garden open. A friendly gesture towards the townspeople, I thought.

A young couple holds hands, two boys run with youthful energy drawn from the first spring days, a family herds toddlers — all in the company of Greek philosophers carved in marble, an elephant and a crane cast in bronze. The greening shoots of tulips promise a blanket of color for Easter. The pergola frames the copper steeple of the new Lutheran church in the distance, and the massive tower of the First Christian Church soars above the slate roof of the Irwin mansion.

Victorian cast iron fence (15).

Cummins Engine Company, Inc. - Components Plant courtyard.

While I was sitting in this oasis of serenity, my mind traveled in space and time and transported me to my favorite Florentine garden, Gamberaia. I found myself in Renaissance Italy trying to imagine the man who had operated a general store in Indiana in the mid-nineteenth century, whose son built all this. An Italian garden here in Columbus, next to a Finnish masterpiece! And then all that followed, built by the best America had to offer. Did this garden inspire Columbus, or had the town's creative energies crystallized on this spot?

I had asked myself a question that has no answer. We know only that the early builders came from England, Prussia, or Ireland via Pennsylvania or Kentucky and that their successors hired artists who had been born in Florence, Dublin, Riga, Canton, Buenos Aires, Houston and Manhattan. A typical American story, yet Columbus is certainly not typical. Maybe it is the American Dream come true: people escaped suffocating cultures and drew vital energy from the oxygen-rich atmosphere of the new land. The fathers, who had worked for popes and princes, had set standards for the sons. The sons came here to realize their frustrated aspirations for themselves and their descendants.

Eliel Saarinen, who came from Helsinki, designed the First Christian Church. Sitting in the Irwin garden on this March morning, I admire its beauty made alive by Sunday worshipers. In the shadow of the belltower, yesterday's snow caught in the grass brings out the fine tracery of the pavement. As I walk back to town I see the loving brickwork of the old City Hall aglow in the morning light. The architect, justly proud of his work, engraved his name in the cornerstone. Washington Street shows its pride, too. The vertical rhythm of the Victorian facades draws the eye to the old courthouse. The streetscape is richly textured and harmonious, with just the right amount of individuality in ornament and variety in size. It reflects the exuberant spirit of its time tamed by the discipline and self-control of a small town. The discipline endures. The courthouse is respectfully restored, mirrored now in the glass curtain wall of the new City Hall, a prismatic image in a kaleidoscope. The local newspaper, *The Republic*, watches over the public forums from a strategic location.

Now the farmer need not wait for the yearly fair, he brings his son to visit Tinguely's sculpture in the Commons for more fun than any ferris wheel. A sharper boy will recognize its spinning wheels, as parts of an old combine.

The magic of wheels has had a grip on Columbus. While another farm boy was hard at work in Detroit to put America on wheels, here the manufacturers of the "Hoosier Boy Corn Plow" built an eight-wheeler, named "Octoauto," a local banker put an interurban tram system on rail, and his chauffeur took out a patent on an engine pioneered in Germany by a man named Rudolf Diesel.

This building genius left more than a stable architectural heritage. The farm community took up the nineteenth century's industrial challenge and rolled into the twentieth on iron-wheels. In 1930 Clessie L. Cummins surprised New York in his diesel powered car, driven from Indianapolis at a fuel cost total of $1.38.

A reading of Bartholomew county's history with its eloquent brief biographies illuminates the character of the people who made this town a landmark.

Here are sketches drawn by a biographer in 1888:

James N. D. Reeves, founding member of Reeves & Co. "....Like many of the substantial self-made men of the day, Mr. Reeves' youthful days were spent amid the active scenes of the farm, where were learned those lessons of industry and self-reliance by which his subsequent life has been characterized."

Rev. Z. T. Sweeney, minister of the First Christian Church. "...As a public speaker he has few equals.....he has a happy faculty for illustration, and can paint in words anything in nature from a sunrise to a thunder storm with wonderful facility and beauty. And yet his ornamentation does not detract from the strength of his argument nor from the soundness of his logic. With him the truth is never sacrificed for beauty."

Bartholomew County Courthouse reflected in the curtain wall of the Columbus City Hall.

"With him the truth was never sacrificed for beauty."

Meaningful words about a man, the Reverend Zachary T. Sweeney, who must have exercised a strong influence on his townspeople.

One may speculate about the history of commitment to intrinsic values, and resistance to superficiality as a legacy from such a leadership.

For architects — high priests of beauty, prophets of truth — this is a most serious quandary to face.

In the past it was easier for an architect to harmonize with a desirable environment once the high standard of quality had been set. A limited choice of building materials, often local, and of technical solutions, a slower pace, less pressure to be different lends a certain natural unity to the realm of older buildings.

It is a more difficult problem to reach a mutually respectful coexistence among modern buildings. Not only have the choices of materials and techniques multiplied, but a faster turnover in trends and styles both in architecture as well as in the behavior of its users has made the appearance of continuity an elusive goal. But perhaps the hardest proposition in the case of Columbus was to moderate the highly individualized approaches of architects coming from distant places with varied backgrounds.

And the fact that a commission in Columbus became a high prestige challenge to a profession where humility is a virtue rarely rewarded did not make things easier.

The visitor must evaluate the success of the effort to create here a place of harmony and well being.

The camera, or rather the man behind it, can be biased.

Details from the past exemplify a tradition of quality.

*301 Washington Street (former Irwin Bank) framed by the
Commons-Courthouse Center (24).*

  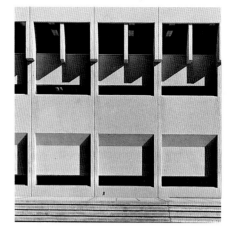

 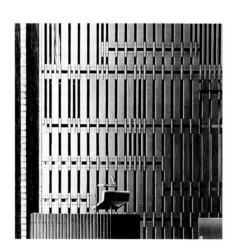 

Contemporary details extend the tradition of quality.

View from Bartholomew County Courthouse Tower—1975 (27).

25

CHAPTER 1

IMAGES FROM THE PAST

Tommy Harrison likes to remember a phone call he got one midnight from a policeman. There is this photographer, the officer explained, with his camera glued to the windowpane of the First National Bank. He has a beard and a funny accent, but he says he works for you and is making a time exposure.

A beard in 1960 was an identification badge in a place like Columbus, and Tommy must have had a little problem. How did he know that this guy he had hired for a day's work was not trying to make a little extra at night robbing banks? But Tommy was sleepy and decided to wrestle with the problem in the morning. Yes, that's Balthazar. He's O.K. Good night, he replied, and hung up. I was off the hook. Still, to cover myself in front of the officer, I swung my Hasselblad around for a shot which had intrigued me for a long time. There in the dim street light over the Art Deco store front was a girl smiling out of the window. Quite an illusion on the deserted main street at midnight! I don't know if the officer was really convinced that I was legitimate, but he rode off, and I completed my shot of the fashion model cutout, abandoned in a beauty parlor long out of business.

There wasn't much to do after dark in Columbus. You had your steak or pork loin at the Palms with a beer. (By then, after two years of coming to Columbus, I knew how to avoid mutual embarrassment by ordering beer instead of wine.) To settle the late dinner, I had walked through the sleeping town with a sense of discovery as my companion. This experience was new to me. I had lived in a small town only once before, in Bayeux, France, a Norman cathedral town where nothing had changed since 1066. Changes brought me to Columbus and there were many over the years. Still, I felt similarities in the mood of these two towns and I could read them better when the streets were quiet.

Washington Street with the building of the Hotel St. Denis on the right—1969 (29).

I usually stayed at the St. Denis when I was in Columbus. With all my equipment, a motel would have been more practical, but I compromised just to be in town. Besides, I liked the St. Denis: big rooms, high ceilings, crisp linens, and a perfect rest despite the evidence that the hotel had not quite kept pace with progress. The black and white T.V. in the parlor was not the latest model. Still, men in shirtsleeves with their hats on kept watching. White straw hats, the kind they stamp out in plastic nowadays.

The men didn't look like guests. They just seemed to have time on their hands. They reminded me of those Normans sitting in cafes near the market in Bayeux. The only difference was that the French talked more, perhaps because they spiked their coffee with Calvados. In both Bayeux and Columbus, the tempo of life allowed time for reflection; time for time itself.

Years after I had stayed in it, the St. Denis was converted into the Cummins Executive Offices by Alexander Girard. It remains a beautifully crafted building. (The less fortunate Belvedere Hotel on Third Street has since burned down.) Girard, with his knack for reconciling the old and new, designed uncompromisingly modern interiors for the Cummins Executive Offices, yet treated the masterful brickwork exterior with a light hand. He also modernized the 1881 Irwin Bank Building.

Attitudes about traditional buildings and environments have changed a lot in the last few decades. Take a look at Washington Street. Judging by the prevailing Victorian character, the street must have developed in a burst of prosperity after the Civil War. From that time to the 1950s it sustained only cosmetic changes — a little art deco detailing here, some clumsy aluminum siding there. Then, in a fit of historical amnesia, major blocks were carved out for the glass panes of the Commons and for parking lots. But in the mid-sixties, when historic preservation became a national concern, Columbus launched a model block restoration, kept abreast of the movement and occasionally surged ahead. Many fine restorations and adaptive reuses are of more recent vintage, and still more are in the works throughout the town.

Several newer buildings fit into the streetscape by respecting their elders' height and scale. However, Columbus is not a self-conscious historic shrine. It is a dynamic, living place with a past it is not willing to erase from the collective memory.

Washington Street detail.

*FIRST NATIONAL Bank of Columbus—1865, renovated
1925 (now Trustcorp Bank).*

The original Irwin Bank building—1881.

A herald of the super graphics popular in the 1970's.

Alexander Girard's Master Plan storefront renovations on Washington Street - 1964 (34, 35).

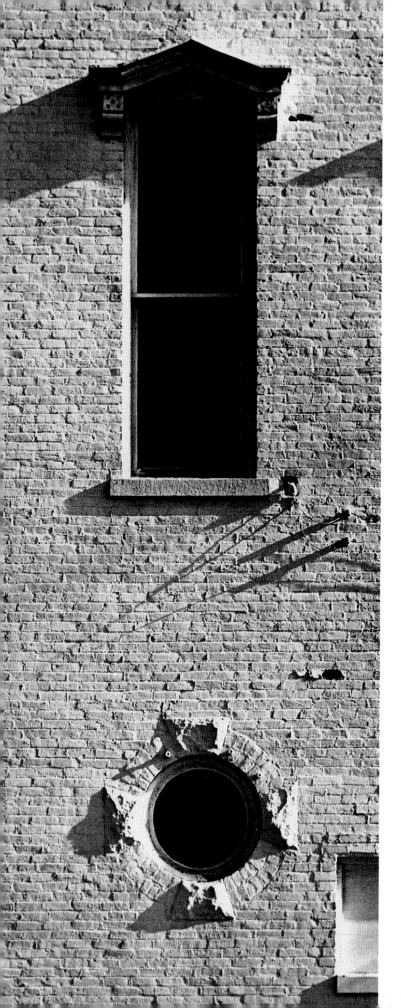

A quiet residential block just off commercial Washington Street (37).

Irwin Home with its Italian garden. The home is dated 1864.
The garden design and house renovation were done by
Henry Phillips in 1910. (38, 39).

Some fine buildings have disappeared over the years (44, 45), other buildings were thoughtfully adapted to modern use (46, 47).

Original Irwin Bank (now the Irwin-Sweeney-Miller Foundations) (46).

Landscape award-winning Franklin Square (47, top).

Detail of the 1903 Power House (now the Senior Citizens Center, renovation James K. Paris) (47, left).

The 1864 Storey House renovation, Bruce Adams (now the Visitors Center) (47, below).

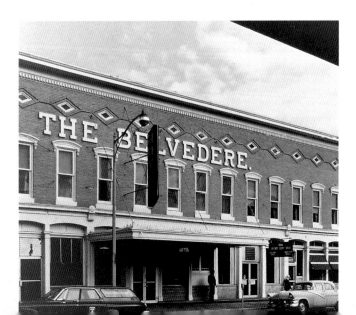

46

WER HOUSE

Garfield Elementary School designed in 1896 by Charles F. Sparrell is under renovation as part of Arvin Industries, Inc. new corporate headquarters.

Interior of the Columbus Inn, the former City Hall, also designed by Charles F. Sparrell - 1895.

Bartholomew County Courthouse designed by Isaac Hodgson - 1874 (49).

49

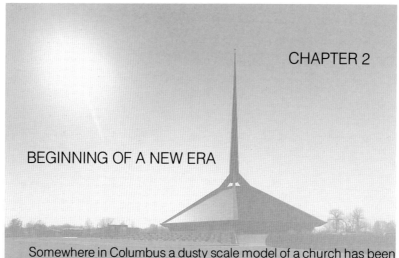

CHAPTER 2

BEGINNING OF A NEW ERA

Somewhere in Columbus a dusty scale model of a church has been stashed away. The model is traditional in design, of fine proportions — the kind of church you can see from coast to coast in prosperous suburbs. It was designed for the congregation of the First Christian Church. It was never built. Instead the congregation now convenes in a church designed by Eliel Saarinen.

History, as one of our famous journalists once said, never reveals its alternatives. Saarinen's church has served the worshippers well for more than forty years but then maybe the traditional version would have done that, too. Yet the choice of Saarinen as architect started something that went far beyond the original intentions. This church stands for values that the best of this town stands for. It marks the engagement of a new era.

When historians select an event to mark an epoque, they do so long after the facts have sorted themselves out. In Columbus there is now no doubt that the new era started with the dedication of the First Christian Church in 1942.

Two famous architects were considered for the commission: Saarinen and Frank Lloyd Wright. The record on both men suggests that the decision was a critical one. Having chosen Wright, two other small towns, Bartlesville, Oklahoma and Racine, Wisconsin became his exclusive domain. Columbus, however, took the path of diversity. Saarinen by temperament favored adaptation over dominance. He conducted the Columbus commission in the Cranbrook spirit of collaboration. Personal expression was encouraged. His wife Loja wove the "Sermon on the Mount" tapestry in the manner of the Art Deco past while the young "modern" pioneers on the team, Eliel's son Eero and Charles Eames, designed details such as the light fixtures, railings, screens, and furniture. The master's hand was steady: such stylistic divergences do not subtract from the church's power and character.

A decade passed after the church's dedication, and with it a generation. In the early 1950s J. Irwin Miller, Chairman of the Board of the Irwin Union Bank, commissioned Eero to design a new building for his family bank. Eero responded with what may well have been the first bank in the country built with glass walls and an open plan. He designed the building during the same period when Ludvig Mies van der Rohe's elegant steel and glass structures were beginning to substantiate the somewhat abstract theories of the Bauhaus. Mies' work in Chicago was seductive and Eero did not resist. He loved sculptural form and always managed to add something of his own. The series of light-diffusing domes in the bank dilute the Bauhaus flavor.

The First Christian Church designed by Eliel Saarinen in 1942 marks the beginning of modern architecture in the community. (51-57).

Pavement and columns in the sunken courtyard (52,56)
Chapel (54) Nave and sanctuary (55).

Not long after the bank had opened for business a need for new schools in the community presented an opportunity to extend the sponsorship of good architecture into the public domain. It is simple enough to see that now, but how many men other than J. Irwin Miller would have recognized that opportunity and seized it? He set up a system for bringing the finest architects in the country to build in Columbus. A committee of two disinterested and distinguished architects was established to prepare a list of six top-flight candidates. The lists were revised for each building so that no architect would get more than one commission. (It didn't work out quite that way — one architect built two schools.) The Cummins Engine Foundation paid the architect's fee. From then on the architect conducted his business solely with the client, with no strings attached to the sponsor. Harry Weese's Lillian C. Schmitt Elementary School, which opened in 1957, was the first in the series and it proved the idea would work. More schools started to rise out of the ground.

In private Mr. Miller was absolutely comfortable with good modern design. Eero Saarinen built a splendid home for him in Columbus as well as a summer house in Canada. Mr. Miller used his influence wisely in building for his bank and for Cummins. His experience of architecture, his sound judgment and his conviction that quality is cost efficient made him a most articulate patron and client. He felt deeply committed to his home town (which in those days cut a rather stagnant image, despite the few progressive buildings) and to its citizens. Having set in motion an ambitious program of public building, he removed himself quietly to the sidelines and watched to see what would happen.

Because I was interested in urban problems and believed in the merits of planning, Mr. Miller puzzled me. Why shouldn't a man with ideals, qualifications, and means initiate action to improve the town? Why wouldn't he develop a plan and then implement it? When I posed this question to Mr. Miller, I used the Medici example in Florence to dramatize the possibilities. Mr. Miller responded thoughtfully, lucidly, with a resounding vote for democracy. Improvements must come from within, he said, not from above. He expressed a true humanist's confidence in education, in the self-correcting process, the process being more important than the product. He considered architecture as part of the educational process. He advocated patience, trust and faith.

I was young and impatient. I thought he was missing an opportunity to make a great place out of this sleepy little town.

The school experiment matured into a school program. More new schools were built by more architects with different approaches and different responses. The school buildings themselves became part of the curriculum. Eleven architects built twelve schools in Columbus. They varied from pavilions set in parks like the McDowell Elementary School, to the introverted and disciplinarian Northside Junior High School. Lincoln Elementary by Gunnar Birkerts is a delicately scaled, compact urban school, while John Johansen's Smith School is fondly nicknamed the "cattle chute" because of its steel ramps.

The Fodrea Community School, next-to-last in the series, was designed with the participation of children and their parents, some of whom very likely recently graduated from one of the earlier schools. I am convinced that it could be demonstrated that the generations who have gone through the new schools demand better quality from architecture than their predecessors. They have learned to expect a lot from a building and when their expectations are met they work to maintain that quality.

Eero Saarinen designed the Irwin Union Bank & Trust Company building in 1954. J. Irwin Miller encouraged a bold contemporary concept setting a tone for the future (58, 59).

The Irwin Union Bank & Trust Company's building program continued in the pioneering spirit.

An addition to the central office was designed by Kevin Roche John Dinkeloo and Associates - 1973.

State and Mapleton Streets Irwin Union Branch Bank, Paul Kennon, Principal Architect, Caudill Rowlett Scott - 1974 (61, top).

Irwin Union Bank, Eastbrook Branch, Harry Weese - 1961 (61, bottom).

Lillian C. Schmitt Elementary School, Harry Weese - 1957. It was the first in a series of schools built with the assistance of the Cummins Engine Foundation.

The Northside Middle School, Harry Weese - 1961 (63).

The Mabel McDowell Adult Education Center (originally an elementary school) John Carl Warnecke - 1960

Parkside Elementary School, Norman Fletcher Principal Architect, The Architects Collaborative, Inc. - 1962 (65, top).

Sculpture: The Family, Harris Barron - 1964 (65, bottom).

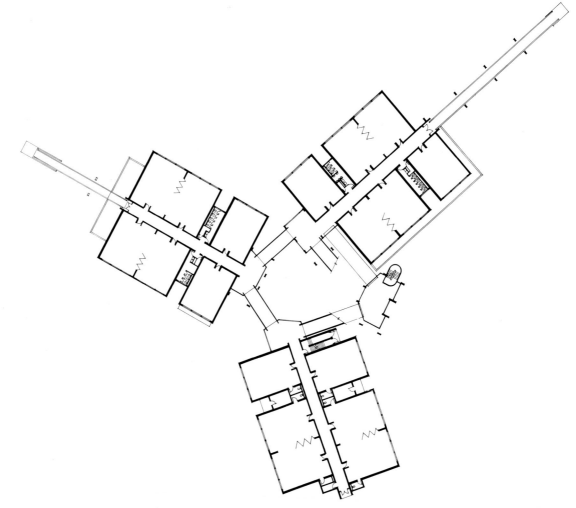

L. Frances Smith School - 1969. John M. Johansen's controversial scheme delights the children with its ramps and prime colors. Courtyard and plan (66).

Southside Elementary School designed by Eliot Noyes, originally a junior high school, contains a courtyard with a skylight - 1969.

Lincoln Elementary School, Gunnar Birkerts met the challenge of a tight urban site with a solution to assure the children's safety from traffic - 1967. Plan (69).

W. D. Richards Elementary School - 1965. Edward Larrabee Barnes featured shed roofs and clerestory windows (69).

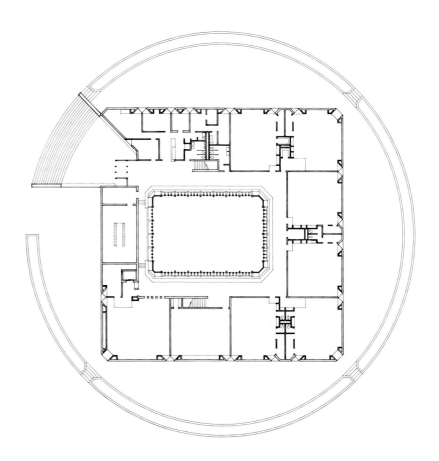

The story of Columbus cannot be told without paying homage to the Saarinens, Eliel and Eero, father and son. Although they designed only four buildings in town, they left a far greater legacy. To date, eleven architects who in some way or other participated in the Saarinen circle have been responsible for some thirty designs for new buildings, additions, or renovations. Those numbers do not include Charles Eames' furniture or Dan Kiley's enchanted landscapes or, for that matter, my own photographs because I, too, once worked as an architect in Eero's office.

In 1922, years before he ever heard of Columbus, Indiana, Eliel Saarinen was at the height of his career in Finland when he submitted an entry to the *Chicago Tribune* tower competition. Though his modern design came in second — a conventional Gothic tower won and was erected — it was widely admired and earned him an invitation to join the Department of Architecture at the University of Michigan. Eliel accepted and immigrated to the United States in 1923. In Michigan he befriended George Booth, a newspaper magnate and philanthropist who had a great interest in the arts. The Booth-Saarinen alliance gave birth to Cranbrook, an educational community. Under Saarinen's direction 300 acres of rolling farmland outside Detroit were transformed into a place of exquisite beauty. European artisans, who had been trained in the tradition of the Arts & Crafts movement, helped construct the school buildings and a science institute. This working community, which was joined by the Swedish sculptor Carl Milles, rapidly developed into one of the leading art academies in the country. Eliel Saarinen, its designer and spiritual father, supervised Cranbrook's departments of architecture and city planning. He was one of the most famous architects in America.

Even so, the Columbus congregation's choice of Saarinen to design their new church was an act of daring. Although his work represented the quality traditional in the town's buildings, his modernism challenged other traditions. The conventional design I mentioned earlier would have been an easier, safer decision. But the congregation went with Saarinen and built one of the earliest modern churches in the United States. The First Christian Church, dedicated in 1942, has long outlived its novelty and graduated to the ranks of the classics. Even today no architect can visit, much less build in town, without taking a humbling lesson from this masterpiece. It quite simply set the standard for modern architecture in Columbus.

The first architect to follow Eliel was Eero, whose works lived up to his father's rigorous standards. Eero's three buildings represent the range of his short, intense career. Both the Irwin Union bank and the Miller residence betray the influence of Mies van der Rohe, yet thoroughly amalgamate into Eero's sensibility. The North Christian Church is pure, mature Eero Saarinen. After Eero came the long list of associates who worked in Columbus.

The Saarinens not only built, they made friends. Will Irwin, Columbus' leading citizen and principal sponsor of the First Christian Church, liked the Saarinens and often visited Cranbrook. A close relationship flourished in the next generation between J. Irwin Miller, Irwin's nephew, and Eero. Young Miller had watched the design and construction of the First Christian Church. He had always been interested in architecture. Now he developed a deeper understanding of the process.

Eliel Saarinen: Cranbrook Academy of Art, Museum - Library and Triton Pools with sculptures by Carl Milles, Bloomfield Hills, Michigan - 1942.

It is an arduous task to climb the tower of the First Christian Church, and it is not ordinarily allowed. But it is worth the effort because there is no better vantage point for sizing up the Saarinen presence in town. In fact, scanning Fifth Street alone would do. You could almost call it Saarinen Street. The Cummins complex lies at one end of the street. The Technical Center and parts of the main plant are the work of Harry Weese who is well represented in Columbus. He worked with Eliel Saarinen, was a good friend of Eero, and belongs to the golden age of Cranbrook's history. Down the street the new Lutheran church faces the Lincoln Elementary School, both designed by Gunnar Birkerts. He is an admirer of the great Scandinavian architects Gunnar Asplund and Alvar Aalto with whom the Saarinens had a natural affinity. Gunnar Birkerts also worked with Eero. Close by the tower is the Visitors Center. Bruce Adams, in the Saarinen-Weese line, adapted the center from the old Storey house. Architecture makes for a funny kind of family tree!

Then there is the Irwin Union Bank & Trust; Eero's first work in Columbus with Kevin Roche's virtuoso addition. Roche, who had assisted Eero in the original design, carried Eero's open concept one step further and placed a glass office complex within a glass cocoon which forms a thoroughfare that opens into a landscaped atrium. The block of Victorian facades across from the bank are buildings that were revitalized in 1964 by Alexander Girard, who is responsible for many fine interiors in Columbus. He frequently collaborated with Eero. Further along are Kevin Roche's excellent post office and his equally excellent Cummins Corporate Building. Dan Kiley the landscape architect, whose thoughtful arrangement of vegetation graces this town and helps weave its separate pieces together, resided over most of the planting. He, too, has connections to the Saarinen circle.

But one street cannot contain the energy of the Saarinen legacy. It has permeated the entire town. From my perch in the tower I can see Paul Kennon's colorful high tech Bell Switching Center. Kennon studied architecture at Cranbrook and worked with Eero Saarinen. He has two other buildings in town: a branch bank and the Fodrea Elementary School which has won no fewer than five awards. I can also see Cesar Pelli's shopping complex and the Commons as well as Charles Bassett's City Hall. Both Pelli and Bassett can claim Saarinen-Cranbrook connections. Finally there is Robert Venturi's fire station. He, too, spent a short time in the Saarinen office. Although the influence of Saarinen in Venturi's work is hardly perceptible.

Eero Saarinen's North Christian Church - 1964 (73).

The interiors of the North Christian Church designed in collaboration with Alexander Girard. Plan (75).

Residence of J. Irwin and Xenia Miller designed by Eero Saarinen with Alexander Girard interiors and Dan Kiley landscaping - 1957 (77-79).

Sculpture: Draped Reclining Woman, Henry Moore (78).

This house is the most important example of Eero Saarinen's residential work. Subtle use of light, the white marble and travertine contrasted with Girard's rich, colorful textures and Kiley's formal landscaping make this a serenely classical home.

As I climb back down from the tower, I reflect about my share in this story; 30 years of photographlc witness. I recall my days as an architect in Eero's office. Our experiments with model photography as part of the design process put me on the track of a new vocation.

That experimental spirit, that open-ended approach was characteristic of Eero Saarinen's office. The glamorous General Motors Technical Center had just been completed in the upbeat image of an industry on top of the world. The spirit was infectious. An amazing stream of technical and aesthetic innovation flowed out of Eero's unpretentious, small wood and glass office in Bloomfield Hills, Michigan. The work force was small and came from all over the world. The team labored, sometimes around the clock but always joyously, in a relentless pursuit of excellence. Jobs were pouring in but Eero resisted growth. He wanted to do architecture, not run a big corporation. The pressure was high, the pay low, but the satisfaction and the *esprit de corps* were genuine. We worked hard but we had great parties, with the whole extended family participating.

Eero was everywhere, gently setting the direction of designs and working harder than anyone else. He approached each project with an open-minded, pragmatic, problem-solving attitude, absolutely devoid of dogmatism. His refusal to "toe any party line" gave rise to a variety of approaches or "styles," a situation which disturbed some purist critics. This was, after all, during the reign of the Bauhaus with its captivating, single-minded message. Still, Saarinen's office went on practicing the Cranbrook tradition of cross-pollinating the arts and crafts and kept producing extraordinary designs. History and environment were respected long before post-modernism laid false claim to the discovery of those territories.

The Saarinens found a unique way to generate excellent architecture and many who shared their experience have since left their own traces not just in Columbus but all over the world.

Eero received the commission to build the North Christian Church in 1959. While he was working on the design, he wrote the congregation that he wanted to make a great building "...so that as an architect when I face St. Peter I am able to say that out of the buildings I did during my lifetime, one of the best was this little church..." What a tragic insight this was, for he never saw the completion of the church. His brilliant career ended abruptly with his sudden death in 1961, ten days after he celebrated his 51st birthday.

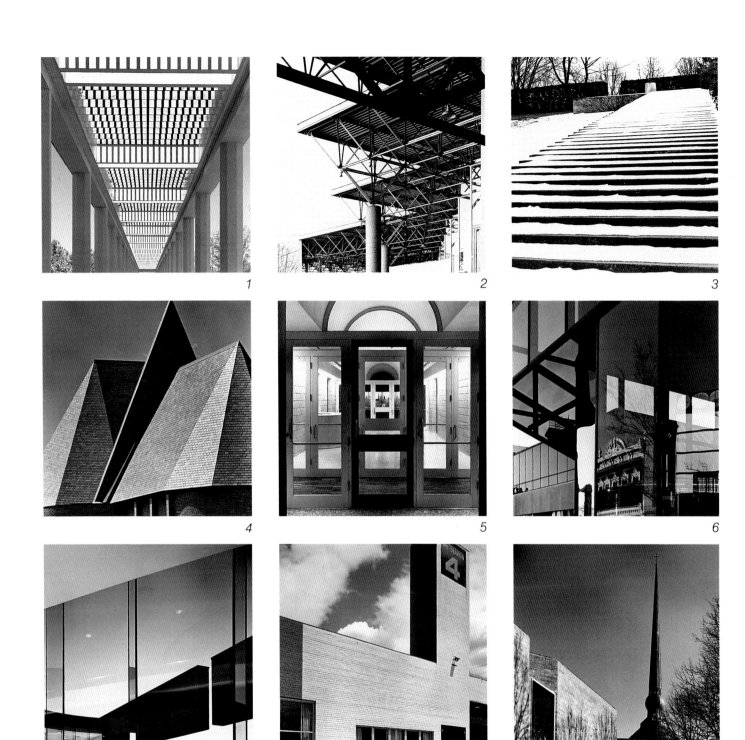

Details from architects of the Saarinen circle:
1. Kevin Roche, John Dinkeloo
2. Paul Kennon
3. Dan Kiley
4. Harry Weese

5. Harold Roth
6. Cesar Pelli
7. Edward Charles Bassett
8. Robert Venturi
9. Gunnar Birkerts

WEESE IN COLUMBUS

I made many of my earliest trips to Columbus to record the works of Harry Weese. I have fond memories of those days, collaborating with pleasant people like Harry and Tom Harrison, who was the officer for corporate facilities at Cummins. Harry's buildings never beat their chests or stood on their hands in an effort to dazzle. They simply answered the needs of body and soul. At the time I didn't consider them very significant achievements, though I did admire the Northside Junior High School.

But times change. "...et nos mutamur in illis." And so did my view of much of the work Harry did in Columbus in the sixties. I don't like to admit it, but post-modernism has probably influenced my perception. Post-modernism professes a recognition of needs it contends were neglected by the modern movement. Post-modernism appropriates unto itself the discovery of the vernacular and the regional, of the environment and of context as well as the rediscovery of history — in principle all worthy ideas. In practice, however, the post-modernists have produced a charade of buzzwords translated into stage-set architecture — all of which is encouraged by the press and talked about *ad nauseam.* To use a metaphor (another beloved buzzword), the post-modernists look like kids who so loved the hobby horse they got for Christmas that they rode it into adulthood.

Now I know Harry Weese would resent any association with post-modernism. But it occurred to me that the post-modernists don't have to look as far back as Palladio for their heroes. They can find one right under their noses. His name is Harry Weese.

Vernacular detail (82).

Lincoln Center, a recreational complex, a gift of the Hamilton Foundation, Harry Weese - 1958.

84

These examples illustrate Weese's understanding of the American vernacular derived from the abundance of milled lumber. His handling of this common material evokes tradition but it does not compromise his modernism.

Canadian summer home, Harry Weese - 1964 (84, bottom). Clubhouse for Otter Creek Golf Course, Harry Weese - 1964.
Lincoln Center interior (84, top).

Pardon me, Harry, if I point out that *vernacular* was on your mind when you designed the Otter Creek Clubhouse and Lincoln Center and that you orchestrated a veritable two-by-four symphony with that summer home in Canada.

As for *historic allusions,* nobody has built a more Romanesque church than your First Baptist Church since H.H. Richardson. You built the Northside School in 1961 when most other architects were turning out schools that looked like country clubs. I felt back home on its no-nonsense premises which reeked of authority. I had learned my ABCs in just such a school built around 1890 in Budapest.

For contextualism, another "discovery" of post-modernism, just look how polite a neighbor the First Baptist Church makes to the Richards Elementary School by employing similar materials and picking up the rhythm of the roofline.

The fact that no one would mistake any of Harry's buildings for what goes under the name of post-modernism proves, maybe, that when one lifts the surface of a worthy idea and probes it deeply and intelligently, the result is not a superficial "style" but good, solid architecture.

Harry Weese has never received recognition commensurate with his achievements. A few years ago the American Institute of Architects bypassed him and awarded their gold medal to someone less meritorious. A great mistake, in my opinion. Maybe this happened because Harry does not fit snugly into the usual categories. He is not a specialist and he has never swum in the main stream. His peers and the press are too lazy to apprehend his qualities.

Church of St. Philibert, Tournus, Burgundy, France, 1009 (88, top).

First Baptist Church, Harry Weese - 1965 (87, 89). Interior.

Northside Middle School interior - 1968 (86).

The First Baptist Church with a Romanesque mood, the Northside Middle School, a reminder of Victorian times, bow to history qualifying the Post Modernists' claim of rediscovering the past.

Weese's neighborly treatment of the two buildings in the 1960's pre-empts the Post Modern clamor about "contextualism". (89).

Irwin Union Bank & Trust Company's, Hope Branch, Harry Weese - 1958 (top). First Baptist Church seen from W. D. Richards Elementary School (bottom).

PROFILE OF A QUIET MAN

The year was 1967. Dispirited by bad news from home and the poor crop of presidential candidates, I had already made the misguided decision not to vote in next year's election. We were living in serenity in the hills above Florence which was recovering from the calamitous flood of the previous November. But news of man-made calamities back home often pierced our serenity: the war in Vietnam, riots in Cleveland, Newark, and Detroit, racial atrocities. It was bad. Such things had not occurred here since the time of Machiavelli.

One day in October I was doing a little browsing at a newspaper kiosk when I noticed a familiar face on the cover of *Esquire* magazine; J. Irwin Miller's low-relief profile, so dignified it could have been minted on a coin. A caption floated above his head: "This man ought to be the next President of the United States." This was not a question. It was a statement substantiated inside the magazine in a ten-page article by Steven V. Roberts. But the title of the article did, indeed, raise a question: "Is it too late for a man of honesty, high purpose and intelligence to be elected president of the United States?" Roberts then nominated thirteen candidates from public life but he chose to discuss only Mr. Miller as the man who best met the specifications. After reading this article, I wished Mr. Miller's candidacy might be real. In that case I would not have to tear up my absentee ballot.

To give but a fraction of the profile of this extraordinary, inspiring man, I am quoting two paragraphs from the *Esquire* article:

"His record apart from business was even more impressive: First layman ever to be elected president of the National Council of Churches. A major force behind its support of civil rights, and an organizer of the March on Washington. Member of the executive committee of World Council of Churches. Served two years in combat during World War II aboard an aircraft carrier in the Pacific. Contributes much of his great wealth to educational and religious causes. An ardent Republican, he gives generously to party candidates, but has voted for Democrats — like Lyndon Johnson. A patron of modern art and architecture, he owns two homes designed by Eero Saarinen. He reads the New Testament in Greek (he also reads Latin) and for years was a substitute Sunday-school teacher. For relaxation plays Bach on his Stradivarius, drives a speedboat, and plays golf on a new public course he recently donated to the city. Married on February 5, 1943, to the former Xenia Ruth Simons, who had been a buyer of iron castings in the Cummins plant. He is tall and attractive, described once as looking like a 'cross between Fulbright and Goldwater.' Father of five beautiful children, three girls and two boys, ages twenty-three through eleven.

Still lives and works in Columbus. Goes home for dinner almost every night with his family. In a recent speech urged fellow businessmen to abandon their role as the 'establishment' in American life and identify with the 'revolution' of the poor.

I began thinking that this could not be J. Irwin Miller. It was Spencer Tracy playing J. Irwin Miller — a figment craftily contrived by a team of highly paid scriptwriters to meet my precise requirements. But a phone call to Columbus assured me that someone named J. Irwin Miller did, in fact, live there. So I went to see him."

Roberts wrote his article in 1967. Now that Mr. Miller has reached his eighties, I am sure the list of his achievements is much longer. I can mention at least one. Three years ago he became the first living American to be inducted into the Building Hall of Fame, an honor bestowed by the National Building museum in Washington.

I have had the privilege of knowing Mr. Miller for over thirty years. I should say, rather, that I have been acquainted with him because of our common interest in architecture since it would be bold to pretend to know this complex, modest and very private man. But you can tell a lot about a man through his accomplishments and in the area of art and architecture alone, Mr. Miller's are overwhelming. Of course his principal enterprise, building the Cummins Engine Company from a small struggling business into a $3 billion international industry, has been — by his own definition — his major calling.

A small episode reveals his dedication to his responsibility as head of Cummins. A few years ago my wife Monica and I dropped into the Left Bank, a popular lunch place. Mr. Miller, who was sitting alone, invited us to his table and proceeded to launch a conversation, which lasted through our meal, about the exciting future of small, high quality diesel engines. It was interesting that he selected this subject instead of our common ground, architecture. It must have been obvious to him that we were ignorant when it came to diesels, even if we were from Detroit. Still, his intensity made his conversation fascinating and he spoke with great clarity on our below-layman's-level of comprehension. We were touched for he had shared something with us; something that deeply preoccupied him when anyone else might have opted for polite small talk.

This book tells something about Mr. Miller's achievement in Columbus and about his love and concern for the people of his home town as expressed by only one aspect of his many involvements, architecture. The quantity of good building in Columbus is most impressive but the process through which it has been realized is more important and indicative of the caliber of the man behind it. I have already discussed in the chapter about the school program how Mr. Miller conceives of improving his town through building. He believes that a good environment exerts a positive force on man's life and that one must arrive at excellence through a gradual, patient educational process rather than by a dictatorship of the "cognoscenti."

Mr. Miller lives his beliefs. He chooses to live in his home town and helps shape it as did his forefathers — but in his own style. There is the Irwin Block, the Irwin Mansion, the Irwin Garden and Irwin Banks all over town. The tallest obelisk in the cemetery bears the name of Irwin. But you will not see Mr. Miller's name engraved anywhere in Columbus. However, his name and telephone number are listed in the directory.

Cummins Engine Company, Inc. remodeled manufacturing plant, an early photograph, Harry Weese - 1961 (92,93), after Dan Kiley's landscaping (92).

Cummins Engine Company, Inc., Technical Center, Harry Weese - 1968.

Interiors of the Technical Center (95, top).
Cummins Engine Company, Inc. interim General Office Building, a conversion from a warehouse, Bruce Adams - 1971 (95).

Cummins Engine Company, Inc., Components Plant, Kevin Roche John Dinkeloo and Associates - 1973 aerial view (top), interior (bottom).

Cummins Engine Company, Inc. interim Corporate Office Building lobby, Alexander Girard - 1972 (96).

Cummins Engine Company, Inc., Corporate Office Building, Kevin Roche John Dinkeloo and Associates - 1983, aerial view. *(98)*.

Main entrance canopy and bronze cast diesel engine (99).

Pergola with the 1880 Cerealine Building (100).

Lobby exhibit area includes an exploded diesel engine in the form of a sculpture by Rudolph de Harak (101).

CUMMINS BUILDS

The Cummins Engine Company's own energetic building program adhered to the same principles that has worked so well in the Columbus school program. A broad range of concepts, architects, philosophies and logistics were dignified in the building and operation of of such complexes as the Walesboro plant, the Technical Center and the new headquarters as well as various health and recreational facilities. Though pragmatic, the architectural process remained faithful to Mr. Miller's overriding criteria: uncompromising quality in the interest of a healthy, efficient business, and respect for the individual dignity of everyone involved. Out of such thinking emerged the bold concept of a plant in a rural area, with parking assigned to the roof so that workers can view the uncluttered landscapes from any point within the plant.

Even temporary solutions were held to the same high standards. Bruce Adams, when converting a warehouse into offices treated the huge space with the utmost care and imagination. His partial mezzanine scheme proved so satisfying that Kevin Roche based his solution for the corporate headquarters on the same principle. Roche wrapped a white concrete colonnade around three city blocks and cut out large segments from the volume to create the generous indoor-outdoor effect that is so characteristic of his architecture. There are three important features to this complex: the thoroughly integrated landscape (an effective environmental gesture), the adaptation of the old Cerealine Building (an accommodation with the past) and, most importantly, the selection of an *in town* site (a decision to stimulate the center of town).

This is the way things were done under J. Irwin Miller's leadership.

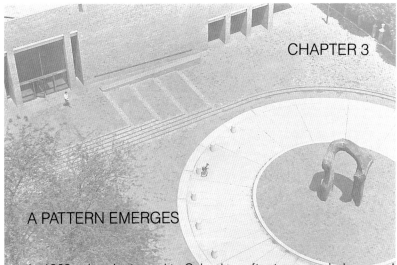

CHAPTER 3

A PATTERN EMERGES

In 1969, when I returned to Columbus after two years' absence, I found the air practically quivering with excitement. I was pretty excited about my assignment. Mrs. Xenia Miller, concerned about all the attention the new architecture was attracting, had asked me to prepare a study of old Columbus and to recommend ways to enhance its values. By then the town already had its model block which stood as an isolated preservation effort. Alexander Girard had suggested a palette of delicate pastels and new signage for part of Washington Street's victorian row. This successful incentive program gave a much needed boost to main street, but a great many of the fine old buildings in Columbus wore the mournful look of neglect. Historic preservation was a new challenge to me and I was eager to get on with my mission. My first objective was to prepare a comprehensive survey.

Along with my study, Columbus was making other moves to protect its heritage. The missing grillwork from the crest and the tower of the courthouse was replaced. 301 Washington Street, the old Irwin Bank, was adapted for Mr. Miller's office. The destinies of the old City Hall and the pumphouse were much debated. My own efforts resulted in an exhibit which volunteers helped install in the new library. I had cast my net widely to capture the images of buildings and places worthy of saving, or at least of recording. The response to the exhibition could be measured by the improvements that soon followed. Franklin Square, the Visitors Center, and a few untended homes all enjoyed facelifts. Columbus was learning to value its heritage, perhaps just a step ahead of the rest of the nation.

All the while strides were being made to preserve the best of the past, new projects were creating the raw materials of recent history. Many of them were public buildings and most of them were concentrated in the heart of town. The Lincoln Elementary School, designed by Gunnar Birkerts, announced the new pattern in 1967. This mature solution to the problem of a tight urban block observed practical requirements as well as environmental aesthetics and still ranks as one of the best buildings in Columbus. Much the same can be said for I. M. Pei's library just a block away where it conducts a civilized conversation with its neighbors, the First Christian Church and a few older buildings. The library and Henry Moore's "Large Arch" anchor one of the most agreeable places I have experienced anywhere.

The Lincoln School and the library got downtown off to a good start in the seventies. Next came a new post office. Thanks to the Cummins

Columbus Post Office Kevin Roche John Dinkeloo and Associates - 1970, the colonnade.

Architectural Program, the U.S. Postal Service broke with its boring precedent and hired a pedigreed architect, Kevin Roche. Then followed *The Republic's* new journalistic headquarters by Myron Goldsmith of SOM. Despite these splendid individual efforts, you could see that Columbus was suffering the same kind of deterioration as most American cities, small or large. In search of remedies, City Hall commissioned SOM to study the problems. As a consequence of one of the recommendations in the report, the town decided to build a central shopping complex on two blocks near the courthouse. The solution, designed by Cesar Pelli, integrates a community center with a shopping mall. The all-glass atrium, which is called The Commons, acts as a link with the main street and houses a variety of amenities including a restaurant, a movie house, an art gallery, and a playground — all centered around Jean Tinguely's magical kinetic sculpture, "Chaos I." Mr. Miller's marginal role in the development of the Commons adds insight to his methods. It was as large a public project as he ever supported but he carefully limited his involvement in line with his belief that the community at large must generate such public efforts.

The downtown revival continued with Paul Kennon's little gem, the Bell Switching station; with Gwathmy Segel's public housing, Sycamore Place; and, later, with the Cummins corporate offices. In 1979, as though to reaffirm that the heart of downtown Columbus was beating strong, ground was broken for a new City Hall.

The prolific seventies also produced a number of buildings across town and in the surrounding regions. Three more schools experimented with an open classroom curriculum — Mt. Healthy by Hardy Holzman Pfeiffer, Fodrea by Kennon, and Columbus East by Mitchell-Giurgola — each with quite different interpretations. There were two new health facilities, Quinco by James Stewart Polshek and the Columbus Occupational Health Association by Hardy Holzman Pfeiffer. Recreational facilities were built to supplement the popular Robert Trent Jones golf course at the Otter Creek Club and the Lincoln Center. Bruce Adams designed a new Par 3 Golf Course Clubhouse, while Roth and Moore produced the CERAland Center for the fitness aficionados. Koster and Associates designed a new wing to enclose the Lincoln Center skating rink.

Once the excitement and novelty of the Commons had worn off, it settled back to prove itself. Similar downtown revitalization attempts to counter the exodus to suburbia have had a rugged time all over the country, and Columbus has been no exception. But it is not the character of Columbus to give up, even on tough problems, so new ideas and different approaches are still being tested.

Whatever the problems, the pattern of pursuit of quality was set. Yet no matter how well motivated it was, some people thought this high class modern architecture smacked of a certain elitist attitude. After all, Columbus was not behaving like a town in the middle of conservative southern Indiana. Because it was unique, the town fell under a journalistic microscope. Skeptics made much of the fact that some residents had ambiguous feelings about all this emphasis on architecture and that a few were downright hostile to it. However, close scrutiny revealed that architects, often nationally recognized firms, got hired for both public and private jobs in Columbus even when the Cummins Foundation was not standing by to assure their fees. When taxpayer dollars were involved, the town made such decisions in open debate. The evidence suggested that the example of quality had taken hold.

Cleo Rogers Memorial Library, I. M. Pei & Partners - 1969.

Cleo Rogers Memorial Library with the sculpture, Large
Arch, by Henry Moore, viewed from Lafayette Street.

Rear view of the library at night (107).

*The Republic, home of the local newspaper, Myron Gold-
smith, Principal Architect, Skidmore, Owings & Merrill -
1971.*

Commons-Courthouse Center, a downtown community and shopping center, Cesar Pelli, Principal Architect, Gruen Associates, Inc. - 1973.

Indiana Bell Switching Center, Paul Kennon, Principal Architect, Caudill Rowlett Scott - 1978 (111-113).
An early view of the Switching Center before the growth of the wisteria. Reflecting glass and sensitive landscaping integrates the building with its neighbors (112, top).
A space frame serves as a trellis for wisteria (112, bottom).

*Columbus City Hall, Edward Charles Bassett, Principal
Architect, Skidmore, Owings & Merrill - 1981 (114, 115).
Painting by Robert Indiana (114).*

Columbus Occupational Health Association, Hardy Holz-
man Pfeiffer Associates - 1973. Exterior and plan (116), inte-
rior (117).

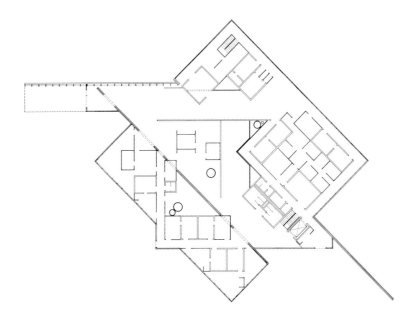

Otter Creek Golf Club, Harry Weese - 1964 (118, 119).
Course designed by Robert Trent Jones, landscape by Dan
Kiley.

CERAland Recreational Center, Harold Roth and William Moore - 1982, isometric drawing (top).

The Center's character reflects its rural setting. (121, top).
Lobby (121, bottom).

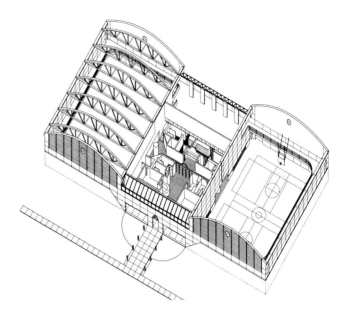

Par 3 Golf Course Clubhouse, Bruce Adams - 1972.

Four Seasons Retirement Center, Norman Fletcher, Principal Architect, The Architects Collaborative, Inc. - 1967 (right).

Quinco Consulting Center, mental health services, James Stewart Polshek - 1972 (123).

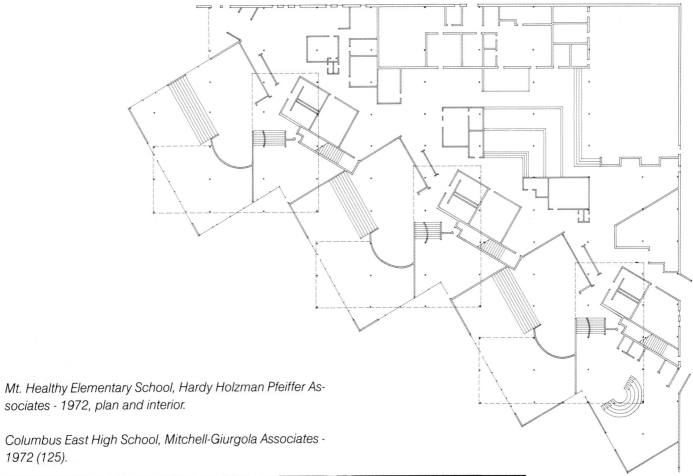

Mt. Healthy Elementary School, Hardy Holzman Pfeiffer Associates - 1972, plan and interior.

Columbus East High School, Mitchell-Giurgola Associates - 1972 (125).

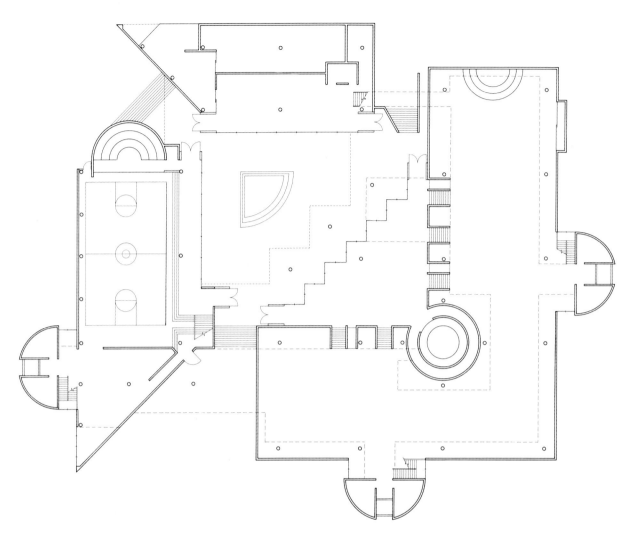

Fodrea Community School, Paul Kennon, Truitt Garrison, Principal Architects, Caudill Rowlett Scott - 1973. Plan (top) Exterior (left & 127, top).

Three schools, Mt. Healthy, Fodrea and Columbus East High School, were designed to accommodate the open classroom curriculum.

Clifty Creek Elementary School, Richard Meier and Associates - 1982 (127, bottom).

Exterior plaza of the Commons-Courthouse Center (128). Jean Tinguely sculpture, Chaos I (top), playground (right), shopping concourse (bottom).

129

Jean Tinguely at work (130, top & 131), detail of Chaos I (130, bottom).

Sycamore Place - 1982 and Pence Place - 1984, two public
housing developments, Gwathmey Siegel Associates (132,
133).

St. Peter's Lutheran Church, Gunnar Birkerts - 1988.
A view from the Lincoln Elementary School (above), Sanctu-
ary (135, top), Ceiling (135, bottom), view from Library Plaza
(136).

Some of the proven urban redevelopment sites, such as the Baltimore harbor or Boston's Quincy Market, may be runaway successes, but by contrast with the low-key natural growth in Columbus, they suffer identity crises which place them somewhere between Colonial Williamsburg and Disneyland. They also sustain a high-intensity, seven-days-a-week, round-the-year industry of the kind that eventually burned out in other less successful sites like "Old Town in Chicago," the "Gaslight District" in St. Louis, or "Underground Atlanta." Here in Columbus, tourists will never alter the pleasing local rhythm. Hopefully the people will see to this. The routine of the workday is different from that of the days of rest. Time is set aside for May Day festivities, grand concerts on the library plaza, admiring the colorama of autumn and the dogwood bursting into bloom on a sunny spring day.

The town reflects the images of its inhabitants in a generous mirror with many facets. Some of those images flash through my mind: the noisy football practice across from the Lutheran Sunday school; a kid sitting on the ramparts of the library, immersed in the private rapture that comes from reading a good book; the lively parade of the latest T-shirts at school break on Twenty-fifth Street's fast food row, strategically located near the Senior High; an old man in his farmer's blue denim shuffling down the mall on his way to Sears with a couple of broken bolts in his hand.

Of course, there have been encounters which do not quite align with those Norman Rockwell pictures. Some time ago Jean Tinguely came to town to construct "Chaos I." He spent months with a welding torch in the pumphouse. He became a fixture around town with his respectable moustache and his black outfit which made him look like an old fashioned steam engine operator. He commandeered the memorable day when "Chaos I" started its hissing, puffing, rattling performance in the Commons to everyone's delight. People from all around the world began to descend upon Columbus. Casual meetings with artists and writers from all over became ordinary events. Architects, of course, were all over the place, maybe working on a new project, participating in a symposium, or just visiting along with the thousands who were starting to turn Columbus into an architectural mecca. The focal point, the Visitors Center where Graziella Bush welcomed tourists with enthusiastic hospitality, became a veritable international crossroad.

Gone are my lone dinners at the Palms and the sensation of having landed on the moon. Gone, too, are the days when Bruce Adams and I haunted the streets in quest of a not-too-square meal and felt lucky if we ran into chef Gregory and got an impromptu invitation. Now Columbus boasts of Walnut Rooms, Hob-Nobs, and Left Banks, along with the ever-reliable Columbus Bar, and the Buffeteria for local flavor.

The Cummins Headquarters is an impressive building. It might even be forbidding were it not for the lovely green peninsula of lawn, fountains, and trees facing the town through a pergola. There are inviting benches too, and not a "Keep Out" sign in sight. Personally I prefer the factories. There are two Fortune 500 companies in Columbus, and as the Mayor Bob Stewart likes to point out, Indianapolis has only one. Along with Cummins, there is Arvin Industries, a manufacturer of automotive parts, and Golden Foundry have their plants right in town. There is something reassuring about a plant within walking distance from home. Bread and security are within sight and there is nothing abstract about how it is earned, when the kids can see from the playground where dad or mom works.

For all that, Columbus is not merely a company town. A certain independent spirit arises, perhaps from closeness to the soil. Farming is still an important occupation. Many people split their loyalties. Tom Bonnell, a Cummins facility engineer, took me out to visit his 800-acre farm on which he works with his brother and his wife who both hold down other jobs. So the man in the three-piece suit having lunch with you at the Left Bank may be in his overalls operating his air conditioned combine that night.

One of the volunteers who worked on the historic show was an articulate young man who owned a small ad agency in town. He was a newcomer, so I asked him what had made him come here and stay. "As head of a large family," he explained, "my concerns are balanced between my professional ambitions and the quality of life. A big city might offer me some career advantages, but they would surely be at my family's expense. Where else can I find a healthier atmosphere to raise children?"

The First Christian Church and the Cleo Rogers Memorial Library dominate this much-loved plaza with Henry Moore's Large Arch in its center. The Visitors Center, the Columbus Inn, some preserved old homes, and thoughtful landscaping are accented by the Bartholomew County Courthouse Tower and St. Peter's Lutheran Church spire in the distance. (142, 143).

The tradition of fine landscaping extends through the private and public domain -- Bradford Pear trees on First Street (144) and the garden of Clarence and Muriel Hamilton designed by Dan Kiley - 1971 (145).

Celebrations: Parade at the opening of the Commons-
Courthouse Center, Street Painting (146, 147).

Photo by Christian M. Korab.

Seasonal Holidays: May Day in Mill Race Park (top).
Balloon sale (bottom), an autumn picnic at Tom Harrison's
cabin in neighboring Brown County (149, center right).

Work and Worship: North Christian Church (150), Columbus Occupational Health Association (top), Fodrea Community School (middle), Route 46 Bicentennial Landscape Project (bottom).

151

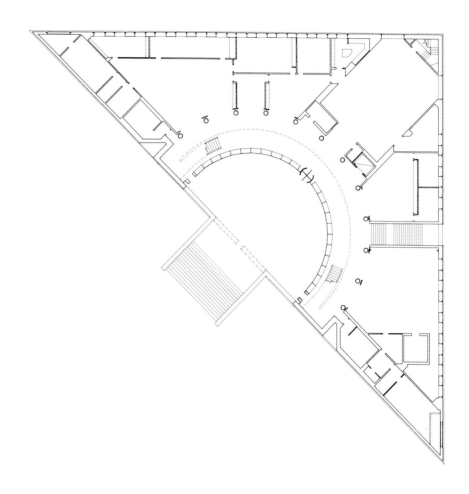

Columbus City Hall (152-157); interior (152), plan (above), curtain wall detail (154) and main entrance (157).

Former City Hall, now Columbus Inn, Charles F. Sparrell, - 1895 (155).

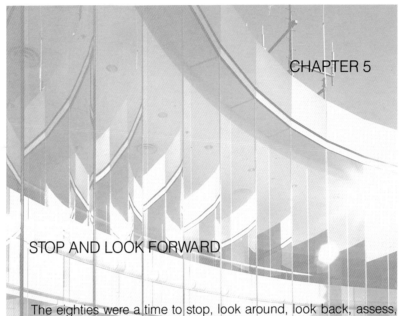

CHAPTER 5

STOP AND LOOK FORWARD

The eighties were a time to stop, look around, look back, assess, maybe look ahead but not too far. A time to gather energy from rest, incubation time for ideas. A time to dream of a future made out of stuff of the past.

Relatively few buildings were built in Columbus during the eighties. The day to day needs had been met, the most important civic buildings built, industrial growth had leveled off, and the population had stabilized.

One new building, City Hall, has a strong symbolic meaning. Not only is it the instrument of urban democracy, but the place where it stands and the date it was built completes a cycle in space and time. Its multi-faceted curtain wall mirrors the 100-year old courthouse.

The buildings were few, but they were important. Along with City Hall, the Cummins Corporate Offices brought much needed energy to the downtown zone. So did Sycamore Place, the excellent public hous-ing complex, St. Peter's Lutheran Church, and Arvin Industries' decision to graft their new corporate headquarters to the long boarded up 1896 Garfield School. There have been a number of new restorations, and a new law enforcement building, designed by Don Hisaka, is currently under construction.

It is a good moment to pause, look around, and reflect on the cumu-lative effect of thirty years of individual efforts. When I first arrived in the late fifties, I found Columbus still struggling out of the nineteenth century. During the next three decades it caught up and became a proud and thriving twentieth century town. But no town is ever completed. It is a living thing, constantly readapting itself to the changing needs of its citizens. Having crossed into the twentieth century, Columbus is now preparing for the twenty-first.

Mothers Day 1989. A group of involved citizens gathers in the Commons to celebrate the theme of a "Town that dares to dream." In comes the next generation. Will Miller, J. Irwin Miller's son, invites Paul Kennon from Houston to attend the festivities and address the audience. He talks about dreams of a better downtown, a better life through a better environment, dreams of the future. One thing leads to another, and before long a forum is organized to gather ideas from the public. The town hires CRSS, with Kennon in charge, to coordinate and interpret the results of this grass roots initiative. A dialogue begins between Kennon and the community and ideas spawn ideas. Focus 2000 was formed in the mid-eighties from a combined private and public initiative to consider problems and project the future of the community. It is now complemented by a new group, Columbus 2000, to implement the ideas. Decisions were made, plans drawn up and the rumbling of the earthmovers can already be heard.

Christopher Columbus' discovery of America will be celebrated in 1992 by his namesake town in the true civic spirit of full involvement with a long list of achievements. They will stand as a daily reminder that the 21st century is only a few years away.

Columbus, Indiana and Bartholomew County
GENERAL INFORMATION

Location: Longitude: 85, 53', 35.8", W
Latitude: 39, 15', 57.7", N
Elevation: 656 feet
45 miles south of Indianapolis
69 miles north of Louisville
78 miles west of Cincinnati
36 miles east of Bloomington

Size: 17.4 square miles

Climate: Four distinct seasons.
January average temperature: 28°
July average temperature: 84.4°

Demographics:(All 1980 figures)
Columbus population: 30,614
Bartholomew County population: 65,088
Median family income: $19,504
Per capita income: $7,895
Racial composition: 97.55% White, 1.57% Black,
.88% other

Government: Bartholomew County Seat
Full-time mayor, 7 member city council.
2nd Congressional District of Indiana.

Economy: Manufacturing
45% of workforce
$510,200,000/year value added
Five largest employers:
Cummins Engine Co. (5419 employees)
Arvin Industries (1900)
Cosco, Inc. (862)
Golden Operations (634)
Interstate Brands (541)
Agriculture
11% of workforce
$37,100,000/year sales
750 farms
120,000 acres under cultivation
80,000 head of livestock

Transportation: Interstate 65
Columbus Municipal Airport
Columbus (City bus service)
Conrail mainline Indianapolis-Louisville

Churches: 109 Protestant, 2 Catholic, 1 Jewish,
approx. 40 other

Media: 1 Newspaper, "The Republic" (circulation: 22,495)
4 Radio stations

Education: Bartholomew County School Corporation:
17 schools (K-12)
Parochial and private: 8 schools
Branch, Indiana University–Purdue University
at Indianapolis
Indiana Vocational Technical College

Library: Cleo Rogers Memorial Library (175,000 volumes)

Health: Bartholomew County Hospital
        Southeast Indiana Stress Center
        Quinco Consulting Center
        Columbus Occupational Health Association

Arts &
Entertainment: Columbus Visitors Center
        Architectural Tour (50,000 visitors/year)
        Branch, Indianapolis Museum of Art
        Columbus Arts Council
        (Supports music, dance, crafts, theater, art
        exhibits, and an historical society)
        Columbus Pro Musica Chamber Orchestra

Recreation: City operated:
        14 outdoor parks
        1 indoor park (the Commons)
        26 tennis courts
        2 pools
        1 ice arena
      3 public golf courses
      1 country club

The list above is selective and certainly not a definitive study. The purpose is to give the reader a feel for Columbus only, as the statistics date variously from between 1980 and 1988. Sources include the Columbus Chamber of Commerce, the Columbus Visitors Center, and Indiana University.

THE MAP OF CENTRAL COLUMBUS

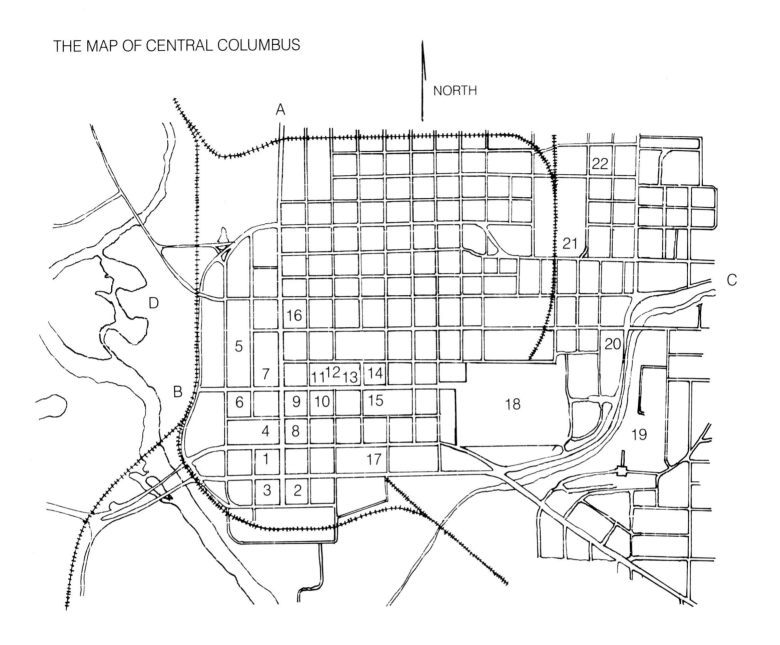

NORTH

1. Bartholomew County Courthouse
2. Columbus City Hall
3. The Republic
4. Commons-Courthouse Center
5. Cummins Corporate Offices
6. Post Office
7. Irwin Union Bank & Trust
8. 301 Washington Street
9. Columbus Inn
10. First Christian Church
11. Columbus Visitor's Center
12. Cleo Rogers Memorial Library
13. Irwin House and Garden
14. Lincoln Elementary School

15. Saint Peter's Lutheran Church
16. Indiana Bell Switching Station
17. Sycamore Place
18. Cummins Main Plant
19. Cummins Technical Center
20. Columbus Occupational Health Association
21. Golden Foundry
22. Arvin Industries

A. Washington Street
B. Fifth Street
C. Hawcreek Boulevard
D. Mill Race Park

SELECTED BIBLIOGRAPHY

Akerson, Alan W., "Columbus, Indiana — An Architectural Treasure Trove" *St. Louis Globe-Democrat Sunday Magazine* (June 3, 1979): 6-11.

Barry, Patrick, "Columbus Discovered," *Discovery* (Summer 1986): 13-19.

Bartholomew County Historical Society, *History of Bartholomew County — 1888.* Columbus: Bartholomew County Historical Society, 1976.

Clark, Robert Judson, *Design in America: The Cranbrook Vision 1925-1950.* New York: Harry N. Abrams, Inc., 1983.

Diamonstein, Barbara Lee, *Buildings Reborn: New Uses, Old Places.* New York: Harper and Row, 1978: 74-75.

Freeman, Allen, "Living In An Architectural Museum" *AIA Journal* (March 1980): 62-71.

Glick, Jean Flora, "Camelot in the Cornfields," *Metropolis* (October 1988): 91-97.

Goldberger, Paul, "Brash, Young and Post-Modern" *New York Times Magazine* (February 20, 1977): 18-31.

Goldsmith, Myron, "S.O.M. en Columbus: el periodico The Republic" *Ianus* (May/June 1980): 47-58.

Jefferson, Jerome N., "The Town That AGC Built" *Constructor* (September 1982): 28-33.

Jeffery, David, "A Most Uncommon Town" *National Geographic* (September 1978): 383-397.

Jones, Susanna, *It Began with Bartholomew: The First Sixty Years.* Columbus: Bartholomew County Consolidated School Corporation 1985.

Knight, Carlton III, "America Discovers Columbus," *United* (October 1984): 60-70.

McCoy, Esther, *Guide to U.S. Architecture 1940-1982.* Santa Monica: Arts & Architecture Press 1982: 84-87.

Murphy, Jim, "Silver Bells" *Progressive Architecture* (July 1979): 66-69.

Pastier, John, *Cesar Pelli.* New York: Whitney Library of Design 1980: 60-67.

Patterson, Ann "Columbus," *The Arizona Republic* (May 15, 1983).

Pulsipher, Gerreld L., Rosenow, John E., *Tourism: The Good, The Bad, and The Ugly.* Lincoln, NB: Three Century Press 1979: 58-60.

Roberts, Steven V., "Is It Too Late for a Man of Honesty, High Purpose and Intelligence to Be Elected President of The United States in 1968?", *Esquire* (October 1967): 89-184.

Smith, G.E. Kidder, "Columbus and its Building Program," *The Architecture of the United States Vol. 2: The South and Midwest.* Garden City, NY: Anchor Press 1981: 230-241.

Sorkin, Michael, "Tastemakers: J. Irwin Miller," *House and Garden* (April 1983): 44-48.

Spalding, Lewis A., "In Columbus, Indiana Courthouse Center Meets The Common For A Striking—Workable—Downtown Mall" *Stores* (October 1981): 60.

Stimpson, Miriam F, *A Field Guide to Landmarks of Modern Architecture in the United States.* Englewood Cliffs, NJ: Prentice-Hall 1985: 134-143.

Takasa, Hayahiko, "Columbus, Indiana: Museum of Modern Architecture—Greenhouse of Modern Architecture" *Space Design* (June 1984): 19-42 (text in Japanese).

Thayer, Edna, "The Gem of Architecture" *Horizon* (April 1982): 24-31.

White, Carolyn Pitt, "Diverse Architecture Draws Worldwide Acclaim" *Arts Insight* (May 1986): 4-5.

MAJOR HISTORIC BUILDINGS AND RENOVATIONS

Year	Page	Building	Architect
1864	47	Visitors Center	James Perkinson. Bruce Adams, Renovation
1871	47	Senior Center	James K. Paris, Renovation
1874	49	Bartholomew County Courthouse	Isaac Hodgson
1881	24, 46	Irwin Management Company	Alexander Girard, Renovation
1895	48, 155	Columbus Inn, Former City Hall	Charles F. Sparrell
1896	23, 48	Arvin Industries Inc., Corporate Headquarters Adaptation to C.F. Sparrell's Garfield School	William Browne
1910	39	Irwin Gardens	Henry Phillips. Dan Kiley, Renovation
1964	35	Downtown Storefront Improvements	Alexander Girard, Master Plan
1972	47	Franklin Square	
1976	23	St. Bartholomew Roman Catholic Church	Bruce Adams, Renovation
1978		Professional Offices	Frank Adams, Renovation

MAJOR CONTEMPORARY BUILDINGS

Year	Page	Building	Architect
1942	51-57	First Christian Church	Eliel Saarinen
1954	25, 58, 59	Irwin Union Bank & Trust Company: Central Office	Eero Saarinen
1973	60	Addition, Central Office	Kevin Roche, John Dinkeloo and Associates Landscaping: Dan Kiley
1958	90	Hope, Indiana, Branch	Harry Weese
1961		Eastbrook Branch	Harry Weese
1966		Taylorsville, Indiana, Branch	Fisher & Spillman Architects, Incorporated
1970		Columbus Center Branch	Donald G. Wood, Principal Architect Taylor & Wood Architects
1974	61	State and Mapleton Streets Branch	Paul Kennon, Principal Architect, Caudill Rowlett Scott
1957	77-78, 81	Residence of J. Irwin and Xenia Miller*	Eero Saarinen Interiors: Alexander Girard Landscaping: Dan Kiley
1957	62	Lillian C. Schmitt Elementary School	Harry Weese
1958	83, 84	Lincoln Center	Harry Weese. Addition: Koster and Associates
1959		Bartholomew County Home For The Aged	Harry Weese
1960	64	Mabel McDowell Adult Education Center	John Carl Warnecke
1961	62, 63, 86	Northside Middle School	Harry Weese
1961	92, 93	Cummins Engine Company, Inc. Remodeled Manufacturing plant*	Harry Weese
1962		Cosco, Inc. Office Building	Harry Weese. Landscaping: Dan Kiley
1962	65	Parkside Elementary School	Norman Fletcher, Principal Architect, The Architects Collaborative, Inc. Sculpture: The Family, Harris Barron 1964
1963		Bartholomew Consolidated School Corporation Administration Building	Norman Fletcher, Principal Architect, The Architects Collaborative, Inc.
1964	73-75, 150	North Christian Church	Eero Saarinen. Landscaping: Dan Kiley

Year	Page	Building	Architect
1964	85, 118, 119	Otter Creek Clubhouse and Golf Course	Harry Weese, Clubhouse. Robert Trent Jones, Golf Course. Landscaping: Dan Kiley
1965	25, 81, 87, 88	First Baptist Church	Harry Weese
1965	69	W. D. Richards Elementary School	Edward Larrabee Barnes
1966		Foundation For Youth	Fisher & Spillman Architects, Inc.
1967	122	Four Seasons Retirement Center	Norman Fletcher, Principal Architect, The Architects Collaborative, Inc.
1967	81, 137	Fire Station No. 4	Venturi & Rauch
1967	68, 69	Lincoln Elementary School	Gunnar Birkerts
1968	95	Cummins Engine Company, Inc., Technical Center	Harry Weese. Landscaping: Dan Kiley
1969	25, 105-107	Cleo Rogers Memorial Library	I. M. Pei & Partners
1969	66	L. Frances Smith Elementary School	John M. Johansen
1969	25, 67	Southside Elementary School	Eliot Noyes. Murals: Ivan Chermayeff 1971
1970	103	Columbus Post Office	Kevin Roche John Dinkeloo and Associates
1971	106	Sculpture: Large Arch	Henry Moore
1971	108	The Republic	Myron Goldsmith, Principal Architect, Skidmore, Owings & Merrill
1972	122	Par 3 Golf Course Clubhouse	Bruce Adams
1972	124	Mt. Healthy Elementary School	Hardy Holzman Pfeiffer Associates
1972	123	Quinco Consulting Center	James Stewart Polshek
1972	125	Columbus East High School	Mitchell-Giurgola Architects
1973	116, 117, 151	Columbus Occupational Health Association	Hardy Holzman Pfeiffer Associates
1973	81, 126, 127, 151	Fodrea Community School	Paul Kennon, Truitt Garrison, Principal Architects, Caudill Rowlett Scott
1973	81, 128, 129	Commons — Courthouse Center	Cesar Pelli, Principal Architect, Gruen Associates, Inc.
1973	16, 97	Cummins Engine Company, Inc., Components Plant	Kevin Roche John Dinkeloo and Associates
1974	130, 131	Sculpture: Chaos I	Jean Tinguely
1978	25, 81, 111-113	Indiana Bell Telephone Company Switching Center	Paul Kennon, Principal Architect, Caudill, Rowlett Scott
1981	25, 81, 114, 115, 152-157	Columbus City Hall	Edward Charles Bassett, Principal Architect, Skidmore, Owings & Merrill
1981	120, 121	CERAland Recreational Center	Harold Roth and William Moore
1982	25, 132, 133	Sycamore Place Apartments	Gwathmey Siegel & Associates Architects
1982	127	Clifty Creek Elementary School	Richard Meier and Associates
1984	81, 98-101	Cummins Engine Company, Inc. Corporate Office Building	Kevin Roche, John Dinkeloo and Associates
1984	132, 133	Pence Place Apartments	Gwathmey Siegel & Associates
1987	137	Fire Station #5	Susana Torre
1988	81, 134-136	St. Peter's Lutheran Church	Gunnar Birkerts
1990	—	Bartholomew County Law Enforcement Building	Don M. Hisaka

*NOT OPEN TO THE PUBLIC

INDEX *Photographic pages indicated inside parentheses.*